four crescents

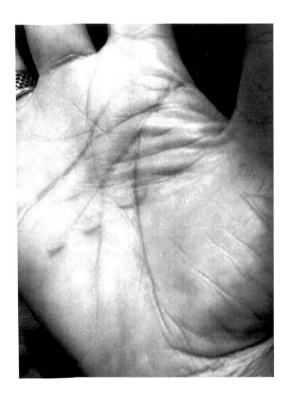

four crescents, the imprint of nails on the palms of fists squeezed too tight for centuries, muffling rage against racism because—as poet norm mattox tells us--- " a Black man in America represents something pent up." But the author is not content to sit on the sidelines---he invites his readers to join him in a war against racism where the weapon of choice is love, and victory is achieved when "no one's child feels like the 'other'", and every mother's child gets home safely. Four crescents encourages us to journey along love's path to create a better future, one in which everyone is able to live life fully and share in the abundant blessings and rewards of the human experience."

- Susana Praver-Perez
  Author of "Hurricanes, Love Affairs & Other Disasters" Nomadic Press, 2021.

four crescents is much more than the musings of an outstanding poet in his prime. It is quite literally a how-to get home safe manual, a mirror into a seasoned soul, and an earnest depiction of a time and place that is in need of a reckoning. Add this treasure to your chest/bookshelf.

- Jose Manny Martinez, poet

four crescents provides an evocative and moving comment on both personal and political issues encompassing love (love lost, love found, love sought after), life and mortality, morality and race, bigotry, and hatred.... demanding a reflection on the inherent complexities and challenges that are intimate, internal, and invisible, and yet glaringly present in our everyday experience. While Norm Mattox expresses himself with grace, sensitivity and a rare honesty, he also expresses and shares a good tongue-lashing with nuanced language that sets forth not only his truth, but a true comment on society. Norm is an intellectual, humanitarian, world-class athlete and all-around loving and lovely human being. His words are careful, focused and meaningful. This compilation of poetry expresses a life well-lived, a soul well-nourished and a perspective which will resonate with all who read his words.

- Ruth C Logan, lawyer

Radical truth-telling and spellbindingly magnetic in its flow, Norm Mattox's raw and rhythmic de-liberation speaks to the burden of having to carry the bridge of racial difference in America. **four crescents** *is poetry that makes every reader a witness, every witness a beacon of awareness and renewed understanding of the deep need for revolutionary joy and love in the face of oppression:*

"so that I risk not knowing where storms blow /my anchor to love is enough."

- Violeta Orozco, author of The Broken Woman Diaries and Stillness in the Land of Speed.

  International Latino Book Award 2022

four crescents

norm mattox

COLLAPSE PRESS

The poem "Barbecue, not a Picnic" is forthcoming in the
2023 edition of *Great Weather for Media*

From an introduction that's a refreshing turn of phrases that open a portal into the conscious thinking of a mathematical mind with a level of fearlessness to use his voice to build "love bridges," from the American fallacy to his truth.

With a beautiful warning of what's to come along this magnetic journey, MATH pulls in readers with elegant wordplay, or saberplay in his case, befitting a fencer and master of words. From its onset, with Default Instructions attached, Four Crescents allows readers a true glimpse into the creative forces that power his pen. Even "against a wall of ignorance," this poet weaves words into weapons, used to fight against the oppressive force, still wreaking havoc on this society today.

Addressing real world issues in the most elegant ways, MATH takes the time to enlighten readers through a series of landscapes - some volatile, others soft and riotous. From a "Cotton Bowl" to "A War on Racism," in which you will find horrors of reality when trying to "convince the ignorant," life in this century looks like "BBQ, Not Picnic," and a great reminder, this "oppressor doesn't ask permission," simply moves through generations as stories or superstition.

MATH opens his heart to reveal a "treasure of vulnerabilities" behind "stubborn built walls" that can keep real emotions trapped in silence. We can clearly see the adoration he has for his muse and reverence he gently places on delicate situations that would otherwise be heavier than "three bags full."

Though this is "barely a glimpse of the expressive words" MATH uses throughout this masterful work, it reminds readers of all levels how the power of words can truly chase away the shadows of doubt and fear. Doing his best to reach blind eyes and closed minds, awaken their senses to the blazing validity that, "unknowing is not enough excuse to sustain status quo" mandates that keep people oppressed in the 21st century.

You will not find pages filled with "quid pro quo promises" in Four Crescents. Instead, you will find poetry speaking the frequency of change without being "full of woulda, shoulda, coulda advice" about possibilities. This is a beautiful revelation that seeds of transformation never stop blooming, they dig deeper - connect to the ancestral essence to plant generational wealth.

As a follow up to his last book, Black Calculus, Four Crescents quenches the reader's thirst for truth, imagery, honesty and a true creative spirit! Do yourself a favor, this version of MATH requires not counting or arithmetic, only your consciousness & ears, to hear the facts, according to MATH. Brilliant!

Elemen2al
Poet, Author, Host, Activist
Elemen2al.com

four crescents

an introduction

when rage is imbedded in the infrastructure of our
community open your fists, look at your palms, how
do you plan on getting home safe?

**fingers balled up
a fist of angst** includes:

- **grief of loss,**
- **pain of heartbreak,**
- **frustrations of inequity,**
- **recognition of chaos (external/internal)**

*provoking multidimensional
evolution, living outside
contemporary traditions*

a fist of angst
balled up in primal screams
howled at the moon
launched into the abyss

the echo of silence
an audible sob
a dovetail on the wind
the edible sigh
a muddy tear slides
down rutted cheeks

table of contents   <u>page</u>

default instructions

**(for disassembly
for deconstruction
for reformation)**

how to be   colored
- watch the commercials
- open eyes wide
- purse red lips to show voluptuous curves
- erase pale, pencil thin lines.
- show a toothy smile   watermelon wide
  while   there's nothing to be happy about
- wear a sweatshirt and a hood in case your
  head gets cold

how to be   negro
- look down   to see where you are
          beneath   being seen,   not quite
  invisible
- "don't speak unless spoken to..."
          like a child   seen,   not heard
- wear a sweatshirt and a hood in case your
  head gets cold

how to be   a nigga
- feel uncomfortable because no one
          wants to be you   or let you be... *you*
- know your place   across the tracks
          at the end of   hope's rope

1

- wear a hoodie in case you head gets cold

how to be   black (a color)
- be dark and dangerous
- be the rhyme that says what you   mean
- speak your mind for free
- say what needs saying
- be air uniforms want to choke from your throat
- breathe life back from the dead
- wear a hoodie in case your head gets cold

how to be   Black (not a color)
- be light that fills dark
- be the hug people reach for
- be waters filling tribe hopes' reservoir
- be the fire in the flame of the phoenix wings rising from ashes   forever rising
- wear a hoodie in case your head gets cold

how to be   human
- compete with gravity
- magnetize love
- attract more love
- give love to your self
- share love you're given
- hold space for others
- find balance in all the betweens
- wear a hoodie in case your head gets cold

a personal dilemma

when 9/11

reminded the usa

that borders were soft

i became one of most

'randomly selected' passengers

in the whole airport.

going from one coast to the other

left to right to left

didn't matter.

i was challenged

to be patient

understanding

i know what surveillance feels like

i could feel the 'check off' look

seven deep in the line

when asked to stand

off to the side

for a 'random' pat down

i had to check my bristle

armor against false authority

and keep moving.

had a conversation with

'sista from another mista'

tellin' me

"i'd stop you too!"

my knee jerk response,

"why?"

i could be from anywhere

over there

be part of a cell

over here

she reminded me

i "looked like an angry Black man

of dubious cultural background"!

i made a conscious effort

to avoid provocative

cultural artifacts,

like necklaces, pendants

hanging earrings,

kufi hats, no berets.

xenophobia continues to be

a tightly wound pitch

that americans

fear any nonwhite member

of the community

not being 'true' American

determined by some

double blind,

double biased,

double standard

survey.

a reflection in a storefront window

the darkness around the eyes

the vertical crease

between the eyebrows.

no light

in those eyes

hyper vigilant

aware of their surroundings

because a Black man in America

represents something pent up

centuries worth of rage

robbed of an open sky

mad in this skin

radiating melanin,

natural sun protection.

always something bad

in the air when the Black man

is breathing it

like a human being

...still a menace

to community and society.

through years of wanting others

to feel safe and unthreatened

by the Black man in the room,

i evolved a look calling attention
to attentively listening eyes.

a smile!
lips relax tight jaws
loosened eventually,
relaxed muscles catch up
with my eyes and eyebrows.
the piercing glare
softened to a gaze
into the in-between space.
holding my Blackness to my head
like a gun wanting to go off
making sure everybody else
feels safe.

working with youth
making sure no one's child
feels like 'the other'
in our class
while i roil and rage

within a system

that maintains 'a gap'

between theirs and ours

with humanity and equity

being fodder for regress

a system that alienates

through cultural irrelevance and

less than casual indifference

for outcomes

measured in data bits

protocols followed

elite bleats, false worry

blah blah black sheep...

an open, accessible face

a patient manner even adults find

safe enough to ask for advice.

when the 'sista from another mista'

shared a meme showing

a medley of Black male faces

i recognized the look.

the rainbow

of brown to Black brown faces

the same blank eyes

the same wooden smiles

they all looked like totems

the look had evolved across my face.

over forty years

of projecting harmlessness

on the media trained

image of a 'house nigga'!

you know

the one

that is under self-control

good at following

illogical and insensitive

patterns of behaviors

because 'that's how we do

things around here'...

hard to resist

the temptation to rip

that placid, subtle

mona lisa grin

offa my face

every time i see

the look like everyone freckled

with salt and pepper hair

of 'dubious' cultural background

and i must.

Resist

burning a bridge

at both ends

while the bridge

is my back.

heart of illusions

better not build dreams from bones
left over from other disasters
— **n mattox**

welcome a trojan heart into my home
   share wealth
an extraordinary love
a treasure of vulnerabilities
  with love   the visa for entry

your first visit   a corner of my eye
sees wood
   a gift to warm
            the hearth of my heart
perhaps   help construct
of a series of bridges   closing spaces
           between our bodies
     looking back
i see kindling   by the door

illusions of a hopeful future
a miscalculation   when one
 love shows up as two   without
  the necessary incantations

a shadow dances between memory
      and possibility
divided attentions   a rival to be unrivaled
    an 'other' love unrequited...

with twenty twenty-one   hindsight

11

i recognize the wood
brought   to the mansion of my heart
flesh of my soul   my home
          as tinder
to be used in case i want to burn
          bridges   in retreat

ashes yearn for company

a partner in life
a trajectory of
happily ever afters

i left with love
i never came home   grief

packed all my smiles
boxes stacked to the ceiling
handwritten labels
block letter kisses
bubble wrapped hugs
closets full of memories

my feet filled those shoes
like a parade of sisters
stand in formation

there's joy in grief knowing that
i'm welcome to visit him
rude and uninvited on a whim

even though i got my own key
i knock every time
confident he'll invite me in.

fingers hearts eyes
read the card
i wrote in long hand

my shadow keeps

the door open, ajar

he's got other things to do
so, i won't stay
as long as
my light

has a place to stand
under the hat
in the closet...
a jar

a new concept on national defense

there are no casualties in a love war
wounds waved closed with a caress

hate and indifference
the only collateral damage

sirenas are the early warning system
calling attention to neglect
and pockets of fear
that could blossom into hate

hate is bored to tears
        bile-filled messages
fall on deaf ears
no one joins their misery

a remedy for   indifference
comes in large doses   of attention
focused   on hurt feelings

self-defense   a self-hug
        fills combatants
with faith and courage
to love their enemies
        to life

differences and borders
are well-manicured fields of creativity

sown
        grown

harvested
by our children's children
...so

the only legacy they know
is love bridges
generations and dimensions
across time and space
a tesseract

with no corners or edges

a new world for our humanity

a smiling totem

silence makes me
a silent target
          - n mattox

fear used to wear my mouth
like a set of false teeth

fear wore the bully hat
          sometimes
fear was my first villain
          sometimes
fear was my neighbor's abused son
          sometimes
fear is the leader of the dog tribe that
          wears white hoods

a false belief that my silence
kept the victim's scent from
mingling with the foul air
sweating off my body

fear recognized my pheromones
the sound of a lamb's bleat
          carried on a breeze
               a full-fledged appetizer
before the main course

when the words in my poetry
connect with the cartilage and sinew
          of a conscious mind
               i see fear mongers

drop their weapons
melt their armor
    dismantle the authority
fear had embedded
       in muscle memory

without fear in mind
i am not a block of wood
i am an ocean

galaxy abyss

words
walk me from a whim
to a whiff in the winds,
to where the sound
of the silent 'e'
splashes in the breeze
of your waving tongue.

'rrrrrrrrs'
run like rivers
and railroads
ferrocarriles
go in all directions
like wayne shorter blue notes
spin spirals.

webs spin,
drunken monkcys
see and monkeys do
from notion to motion.

words
flash thunder
throw down thumbs
drums beat on a virtual screen.
put it down
on some paper
pen
pencil
fingernail in the sky.
a crescent moon hangs

over a midnight horizon.

a word
like an arc of light
connect the two points
i try to marry,
'til death do us parts
of the
same circle
the same pueblo,
the same tribe
of hearts and minds
speak hidden truths
instead of transparent lies.

fingers flash
bring the same fury
desperate to cross
the abyss of ignorance.
especially,
when the hearing
dont listen.
speaking is babble
unless the words
string together
like this.

**breaking down the pedestal of
love's sandcastle architecture**

the tide
     a moat in motion
a swirl of yellow flags
     wash up on the rocks

i entertain overnight overtures
     at the mouth of the bay
     time limited to blueprints
drawn on waterproof paper

where to build home
     futures subject
to sea changes
     rip currents   undermine
dreamy loam foundations

without vision   hope
     at risk of sliding into
the surf
        undercurrents
            undercut
        underground
fiber optic images
          of designer dreams

too many shadows
     in the light of dusk
timing reality   a hazard

a moat misfunction   signals

fear   on high alert
encoded messages
scroll across chicken skin

status quo guardians   suggest
you bring kindling   lay it at the foot
of unfinished bridges   suggest
you collect tinder   no blankets
       for cold hearts

wake dream keepers
       to bring sage
where dreams are created
       the same place
where dreams are treated
       for smoke inhalation

draft EMTs to heal   the wind
    a siren song   clears a path
to collect   the bodies

hire civil engineers to redesign
       labyrinth paths
to a peace of mind

be gentle   with lives
never   lived like this
   the first time

no muscle memory
to remember how
       to get home safe
in a strange land

i forgive you

me   a witness
to wordless discord
        your side and my side
no middle   silence wins
no agreements to make
no promises to keep

you feel   my ignorance of the dis-ease
missing your side by my side
unbeknownst to me   makes it
my fault   not reading the writing
        on the walls of your closet

me   a bystander
to a dialogue
      a hint of your conversation with
a dissatisfied self
      not hearing all the sides

passive aggressive
            versus
stubborn   built walls
we would never get over
dug graves   a refuge from life

i forgive you   for waiting until
your last breath to say, "im sorry!"
i forgive my self   for wondering still
what you were sorry for

marginalized fringes

i am
doubly redundant

let me be
the last
in the door
i thought
was the front door
but when it closed
behind me
became
the back door
'first one through
last one out
last one in
first one out'

which one am i?

strike one: **young**;
college entry at sixteen

when quota is met
margins filled
          back door
used to be
          front door
swings open!

i am the first one
"welcome to the fringes of

academia!"
remedial high school   i mean
city college,   where i can get
"all A's, if you really want
to be successful."

already successful,
      recovering from
a "**three strikes and you're out**"
           setback

form needs only
admissions director's signature
for readmission
to this ivy league school

strike two: **gifted**;
piano performance
competitive fencer

he looked from the line
where his signature was required
back to my face
he saw my whole village
rise up surrounding us   both

before his eyes
i become my tribe
no margins
to fill
horizons stretching away
in all directions
no fringes,

to stitch together
only expanding edges

he can only sign the document
i know his fear!
afraid ima bring in more
...like me

like when scouts
became invaders
became victors
told lies
became the truth
became the history
as in historical lie
written as
'make believe' greatness
to return to

a lie twists
like a scarf
in the wind
too much time
spent defending it
trying to 'remember' it
who cares about omitted 'facts'?

truth stays truth
whether it's remembered
details left out
or forgotten entirely

generations of socialization

liars repeating lies
make it more than myth,
make it harder than concrete,
make it to die for,
patriotism

strike three: **Black**:
self-aware in community;
two years Blacker than when i entered

i know his fear
just sign the document
don't be afraid
when i settle in

i won't treat inhabitants
like people whose past
is forgotten   nor
like people   whose future
needs marginalization

i am nothing like the past
you want us to forget
i am nothing like the future
you want us to be afraid of

Ancestral Diatribe

no one said it was simple
to put your hand on the doorknob
scroll   through the masks you wear
so you can return home alive

revolution is not   a spin through
     your life cycle   a stationary bike
going the speed of breathing
          last breaths

evolution is   change
at the mitochondrial
           layer of consciousness
unknowing   is not enough excuse
to sustain status quo

i believe dawn and dusk are instruction manuals we
never read

we think we know
how to live in   the light
          of day,
how to be light   in the dark
          of night.

emotions   are like unplanned adventures
mind plans   bends time
  plots   a destination
        becomes   a map
crosses   internal oceans
                gets lost anyway

love is a journey   we take to find
      our authentic selves
a reflection   an echo
of a love that resounds
      at humanity's core

      when i dare to be powerful
step into vulnerable
      wipe the sweat from my palms
bring unexpected   to status quo
      speak truth to authority
step into the space that needs
my being   not   my doing

my mind is a heartless voyeur
keeps love in the basement
in a transparent freezer

my mind doesnt love me like you do
my mind makes me the lover in the closet
my mind makes me the   shadow
          under the   door
my mind makes me the intruder on a 'good thing'
my mind reminds me, "you are the 'other guy!'
my mind makes me the 'he' that "has to go!"

my mind is indifferent to feelings
          makes me question conditions
i put   on   unconditional love
my mind laughs at me behind my back,
     scoffing at me with "i told you so" refrains
my mind sounds like a parent
          full of "woulda, shoulda coulda' advice

my mind does not love me like my heart does
          my mind is outside my self
     full of logic and objective perspectives,
anticipates crisis   when feelings
          are considered facts   and
thinking is done with a conscience of heart
conscious feelings   wrestling with
unconscious thoughts
          threaded through double-eyed needles
                    by drunken monkeys

who loves me, reminds me
          i am more than what my mind thinks

i am the revolution in my evolution
i am more than consequences and outcomes
i am an unending sequence of ones and
zeroes
i am a trend of nows that make me present

i risk not knowing   where storms blow
my anchor to love is enough

Mourning Interrupted

driving down hill
you showed up in
the middle of a sky mourning
careful to stay in my lane
keeping my eyes on you

and the road,
marveling at your balance
hovering in the air like that
eyes on me
swooping through my windshield
arms open wide and encircling me
hugging the air out of my lungs

pulling off the road, up on the curb
holding me in a stupor
trying to catch my breath.
drowning in a river of tears
holding on fiercely to the steering wheel
letting go of the fear
that
i would never see you again.

Barbecue, not a Picnic

my only crime
sir,
      was showing up to a picnic
i wasn't invited to

sir,
   my words might come out
     the side of my mouth,
       there's an awkward tilt to my head

but the truth is,
     they're gonna say
    i ran after them, and
  when i caught up to them

      they're gonna say,
    they wrestled the five ax handles,
away from me   from inside my shirt
    they caught the fourteen fists
thrown   from inside my jaw,
    they opened the razor blade
unsheathed   from behind my scrotum

and sir,
     they're gonna say...   to the court
i showed up with this noose
    around my neck   and
i tripped on it during the melee.

i know it's difficult to make a point
   when my broken fingers

are going in ten   different directions
i'm sorry if my voice is a little strained, and
                my words are a
                        little   slurred, but
these last remarks are having
                a hard time getting around
                                this knot in my throat

sir,
        if you put my shoes on their feet
would anything about their story
                about what happened,
        me,   ending up in the tree,
                taller than when i left my house,
        be true,
                        "...so help them god"?

Cotton Bowl : cotton boll

ekphrastic poem
**Cotton Bowl   a painting
by Titus Kaphar**

16   19
     to
20   19
hut hut hike

400 years
                    melanin armor still thick as keloid
scars
          a badge of courage worn
          across generational hard times
wearing different uniforms,
serving the same masters,
astronomically, rich astronauts and
          dead presidents

fields of cotton filled with the enslaved
                    Black Brown bodies filling capital
coffers
          at the foot of one thousand rows
          proud shoulders anchor generations
backs bent twenty hours a day
sacks of fiber
yeah suh, massuh
          three bags   full

football fields filled with the indentured

Black Brown dreams building
corporate stadiums
        making "hand over fist" money on crashing
bodies
passing trauma forward in sacks of tenuous futures
        broken backs strewn
across domed fields
yeah suh, no suh
        no more   bull

oppressor doesn't ask permission

what would it take
to make
you so mad   you couldn't speak
your mind
          that you would
                    make a fist?

what would it be
that makes
          you so mad
   that   you make a fist
          wanna throw
it at some   thing?

what if society determined
          you lack self-control,
make a fist   hold it too long,
must wanna throw it at some   thing
          wishing 'fist-like harm'
                    on some   one?

theyz not gonna
               wanna see a fist,
          gonna wanna
      pre   vent your crime,
squash the will to resist
before you   vent your criminal fist

they expect
their control
is absolute

better control
your self
best move

that fist to the back of your jaw
hold it there   long enough
        for dentist to question
the mound   of pulverized enamel
        piled next to plateaus
where molars   used to stand

better change the dental landscape
            braces and bridges applied
    before bits of tongue are chewed
bloody and they cant understand
why your voice   is barely audible
behind clenched   teeth and pursed lips.

lawmakers wanna
put a rope   around your voice
        like   judicial and penal systems
reset triggers 'impersonating'
land mines   hidden   around red lines
drawn in quick sands   surround an island

 an oasis   an 'other' land
  tribe   community
    where gentrified
otherwise known as   reverse 'white flight'
brings to memory   a white wash
        is ethnic detergent

if i go first

she will mourn me
until she can curl her ribs
into fingers interlacing a hug

feels like a place she can call home

true and devoted
with an unquenchable hunger for love

as much as
she needs is
as much as
i want to give her

family gossip
whispers loud enough to hear
she uses me
digs into my silver
waits on my gold

how wrong they are

she is chained
to the mine of love
that is mine alone

arms to hold
breath to breathe
love to fulfill her addiction

i am the drug

withdrawal will not
undo the mourning
suffering will be
in the arms of the chauffeur
driving my ashes
to the ocean

a war on racism

would a leader dare
to declare war on racism?
where are the volunteers?
will there need to be a draft?
how will there even be sides?
what terms
        will couch the lies
that will convince the ignorant
leave the dormant sleeping
that the lie is just,   good
and worth dying for?

what separates us
when there are no more middles?
haves   versus   haves not?
got   versus   getting got?
ousted versus gentrified?
thems that's thriving
        versus
thems that's surviving?
a runaway capitalist dream
        versus
a tsunami socialist nightmare?

who will be the patriots
in the war against racism?
are we the ones
they've been hoarding
their 'right to bear' arms for?
will there be insurgents?
will refugees find haven

in their homes?
or will refugees
become rebels
that become terrorists
whose cause is to disrupt
the status quo of the other?
how will you talk
with the veterans
that defended the losers?

all of us are tainted by difference.
none of us is the same.
even as twins
we are still different.
it will come down
to a war on racism
not between
Black or white,
but between
the human race and
an inhuman race.

Tumbling Walls

i want my poems to be timeless
          reality reminds me
      i am barely a glimpse
      of the expression
  of words   especially since
now only reaches
            to the horizons

pages flame with passion
      that consumes a forest
fingertips crumble   like cigar
                   a
                   s
                   h
typing words
      that would blister my lips
and   singe my mustache
if I speak them   into ether   must read
them
      must hear them read

the form of the stanza   follows
      the curves of my heart   traces
the angles of my bones   swinging
on   hangers   in the closet
      on the page   you see the elegance
in my caesura,   eyes shift through
blank space   at the intended pace
      the gravity drop after the
               line break

while my silent pause
                    makes you uncomfortable
                i'm waiting for the echo of
your last thought to
            land on all the places
                    that need to listen

while my profile
                            assumes the mirage of
calm
i am the only witness
            to the tremor
        shaking my foundations
            tumbling the walls   and trap doors

that kept me safe   from my self
in the mansion   housing my breath

no one imagines the roar
            of traditional pillars   tumbling from
attic to basement   the internal
reclamation of space
repurpose the parts
                    redesign the original creation
            longing for a place inside my skin
i can call home.

hashtag throwback thursday

a few lifetimes ago

mt tamalpais was
just over my head,
horizons fell away just
beyond my fingertips,

looking forward

i didn't see the chaos
regurgitate itself living...
no, not living   life
decomposing in fronna me

i didn't imagine the chaos
inside me,
cells composing shadows
on shining paths

rage smolders on
the shoulders of my byways...
heat waves,
          outrage,
                    memory banks the
          tinder box,
     self-immolation plus
          spontaneous combustion

i didn't see the phoenix shed
fear of feathers on fire
knew life on this path

was gonna take off...

ashes in my wake

four crescents

imbedded in the palm of your hand   a streak of
violence
yellow flashes   before red pumps   against
clenched arteries
feeling pressure build   with each mouthful of
mediocrity
take a deep swallow of pride so as not to humiliate
hope and integrity

tradition of winning 'fixed' by threats disguised as
quid pro quo promises
cards dealt   from the bottom of the pile   a clown
with a red tie and pointy hood
fails to stay hidden,   falls out of the deck
during the shuffle
counting on a trump to win   over the face card

dog eared lies exposed to light of truth   lying
tongues burn on a slow rotisserie
blistered lips read captions   in the dark
hyena news slither through
gap toothed smiles   sneers barely hidden
condescension unfurls like a flag
pulled over wool laden eyes

a powerless fist pounding itself bloody   against
a wall of ignorance
porous to lies and deception   yet impervious to
rational thinking
while truth is the renegade   looking for refuge
          hiding in plain sight

a 'wanted' poster crumpled in the clutches of four
curled fingers while

a thumb stands guard against the mob looking for
truth to hang by a thread

my skin, wild seed

(after octavia butler)

no longer a wild seed,
i am the flower
that never stops blooming

what skin gets
me where i can't go as i am?
do i wear leopard's spots

to hide in this jungle of men?
do i flap a bird's wing
to cross the sky?

the skin of a jackal,
invisible until the trick is turned
and the carcass still moves

the hyena laughs
nervously at nothing funny
a show of teeth, a smile

a grimace at an unconvincing lie,
like fingernails scratching
on a black board

me, one of the kool-aid
drinking base wishing to death
the snake oil salesman could twist

genie out the bottle,
put me behind the mirror

show me unseen sides of my self

Norm Mattox is a poet, returning to New York, after raising a family, and "growing up" in San Francisco for over 30 years. He served as a bilingual educator in the public school system of San Francisco Unified School District. Though retired, Norm is a teacher ('maestro' in Spanish) for life. His next journey for teaching and learning is through the voices in his poetry that tell a story of love in a time of struggle and challenge.

Norm has shared his poetry as a featured reader and at open mics around the San Francisco Bay Area, select venues in New York City and other parts of the world across the 'zoom universe'. Norm's poetry has been published in two chapbooks. his first collection is titled, 'Get Home Safe, Poems for Crossing the Community Grid'. Norm's second chapbook length collection is titled, Black Calculus, published in 2021 by Nomadic Press.

Letters for the End Times

    Collapse Press is a small literary publisher specializing in poetry and prose by authors, established and new, whose work addresses the current social atmosphere of a society in turmoil and on the verge of transformation.

OTHER TITLES AVAILABLE FROM COLLAPSE PRESS:

Unit of Agency by Richard Loranger

Death Haiku by Missy Church

Find Me In The Iris E.Lynn Alexander

Splinters by Han Rascka

www.collapsepress.com/books/

Titles Forthcoming from Collapse Press:

Letters for The End Times (Anthology)

Thawing by Taneesh Kaur

COLLAPSE PRESS

https://collapsepress.com/

Made in the USA
Middletown, DE
13 August 2023

36663215R00046